My Startup Diary

ELINA ARPONEN

Yritystutka Oy
Helsinki 2026

ISBN 978-952-88-1734-5 (paperback)
ISBN 978-952-88-1735-2 (hardcover)
ISBN 978-952-88-1736-9 (EPUB)
ISBN 978-952-88-1737-6 (AZW)

Cover art by Laura Wallo

Book version: 1.0 – April 2026

To Ville-Kalle, Amos, and Ava:
You give life its meaning and purpose.

CONTENTS

FOREWORD

This book tells the story of Tribe Studios (2010-2015) as I experienced it at the time and what I learned from the adventure. Tribe Studios was a Finnish, and thus European, startup in the gaming sector. We journeyed from a B2C business model to B2B software. We tested multiple funding avenues and partnership models, often being the first to try something new.

A few years after the acquisition of Tribe Studios, I founded my second startup, Quicksave Interactive, which I am running at the time of this book's publication. We are building a tool called PlayablesAI. My two co-founders now are Ville-Kalle and Tiki, who were already part of the Tribe Studios team.

I don't foresee leaving the entrepreneurial journey—nor do I want to—anytime soon.

The majority of this book was written in 2015 and 2016, but I never published it because I lacked connections to the book publishing community. I also lacked the time to create those connections. What I needed was someone to review and refine the book for me. I had decided to write it in English, which is not my native language. Now, in 2025, I have that personal help in AI.

I hope you enjoy this glimpse into the startup world. Whether you aspire to embark on this journey or are already navigating its challenges, I hope you find some helpful insights to lighten your steps.

Looking at this material now, nine years after it was written and more than ten years after the events took place, it feels like my first startup journey was even faster than I remembered. There are many lessons I've been able to apply in my second startup, but three stand out as clearly different from the first time:

- ✓ Independent self-image: Your startup and you are two separate entities. This can get blurred when you're deeply immersed in the company. It's most visible in how dependent your personal income is on the business—when the company has money, you can pay yourself; when it doesn't, you can't. Beyond finances, it also means maintaining a life outside of work. If your identity becomes too tied to the startup, you may not see the path forward as clearly.
- ✓ Patience: Things take time, and you can't always speed them up to your liking. Startups need a sense of urgency and must move fast—that's your biggest advantage over larger, established companies. However, it's still a marathon, not a sprint. You may wish things happened yesterday. Remember, it will happen, in its time, soon.
- ✓ No impostor syndrome: I grew out of it during my first startup. When you've handled enough tough situations, you learn to trust yourself to tackle the next one—whatever it turns out to be. Bring it on! I'll deal with it.

Of course, when starting a second startup, you also begin with an existing network of people. This is a tremendous help in everything. Additionally, the Finnish/European startup scene has evolved in leaps in the past ten years. There are a lot more VC funds, for example—if not yet quite on the level of Silicon Valley.

PART I BASIC STORYLINE

Dear Diary,

After the events have happened, it is easy to bring out structure. The cause-and-effect chain seems clear, and everything makes sense. But this clarity only emerges in the storytelling, in our description of the events. There are always many ways to tell the story. "Winners write the history," and that is true. By writing history, we shape what exactly happened. It's like in quantum mechanics, where a particle's past can be changed by the measurement done to it in the future.

What then is the role of human action? Are we all but left to the mercy of chance? On the contrary. Our actions today can shape everything, even the past. It is important we keep working to shape our shared story. Everyone gets lucky chances; what we need to learn is to grab them. It doesn't matter where you start; you can always take the next step for the better.

Elina

Tribe Studios was functioning from the 21st of August 2010 until the 31st of May 2015. That makes it a little less than five years but saying 4.8 years is cumbersome. So I'm going to abbreviate that to five years. In fact, I had started to do some groundwork already in the spring of 2010, so five years is very close to the mark.

It is possible to divide this time into five phases or pivots, and that's what I'll do. The phases were not equal in length, but it makes more sense to describe a startup by its business strategies than by calendar years.

1. STRATEGY: WEB GAME

Startup Sauna

Tribe Studios got started at our kitchen table. A group of friends and game industry colleagues happened to gather around that table after a game of floorball. I myself was not at that game, but everyone else was, and since it was our kitchen table, I was there too. (A large part of our company has been playing floorball together ever since.)

But that was really just a gathering, and it was certainly not clear if we could go ahead with the plan to found a company. However, the basic premises were set: we had a good team with complementary skill sets. I had (scantily) the most management experience, and I was the only woman, so it made sense PR-wise that I would be the CEO. (Perhaps I also had the least skill in other areas like code and graphics.) One great asset I had at the time was that I had time. I had been laid off from my previous job as Technology Team Manager at Digital Chocolate with a severance package. I was an ideal candidate to start digging into the practicalities of making the company happen.

This was at a time when founding a startup was not yet

fashionable in Finland, and new game companies were not that common. It was the age before the global successes of Angry Birds and Clash of Clans.

In the summer of 2010, we had another meeting at our summer cottage. We decided upon the name of the company and the type of game we would be creating. We also had to formalize the company so I could start to seek funding, so we filed the papers with the Trade Registry.

Then came the decisive moment during our summer trip when I had a long talk with my husband and co-founder, Ville-Kalle. The company was not going to happen by one person only. Unless he took the jump and resigned, it was not going to happen. The next Monday, he resigned. After that, one by one, all the other founding members resigned too. That kind of describes the role of Ville-Kalle pretty well. He wears many hats, but mostly he's this invisible glue that just keeps things rolling in the right direction through all kinds of feats of strength.

The autumn continued with others working out their resignation periods (some of them three months long). I was negotiating our first funding from Tekes (Finnish governmental funding agency for innovation and technology, that is today called Business Finland), which required us to have a minimum of 30% of our own equity capital. All founders agreed to contribute a sum, and there were family members and a friend from the industry joining this round. However, the negotiations with Tekes were taking a long time and stalling every now and then.

Then our advisor (whom I had met at an event organized by ArcticStartup and managed to convince to support us) told us about this accelerator program called Startup Sauna(*). I looked it up, and it didn't seem like a fit. It looked like something meant for students only and very public. We'd have to talk openly about our ideas for the games. How stupid was that? Someone would immediately steal the great idea.

Luckily, I chanced upon this advisor again at an IGDA (International Game Developers Association) bar night. He asked me if I had already applied for Startup Sauna. I had not. He told me quite clearly that if I didn't, that would be the end of our advisory relationship. The deadline was that night at midnight. So I went home, took the leap, and applied.

It turns out Startup Sauna was a really good thing for us. It was the best "Silicon Valley style" startup accelerator in the Nordics and Baltics. We were in their second batch of startups ever. We knew how to make games when entering, but that was our crash course in running a startup.

We ended up winning the batch and got some local fame for it. The prize money itself was only 5,000 euros, and not a single professional angel investor showed interest (the times were too early for that). However, the following week, things suddenly sped up at Tekes, and they gave us the green light for funding. We were funded for the next six months and ready to roll!

(*) The first two batches were called Bootcamp, and this being the second batch ever we in fact attended Bootcamp. Soon after, the program was rebranded as Startup Sauna. Years later, the accelerator itself was discontinued, but the name Startup Sauna still remains as the name of the startup space at Aalto University. Other accelerators continue to operate at the Startup Sauna premises.

Alpha Build

So we started building Stagecraft: Velvet Sundown. Stagecraft was the calling name for the gameplay style of multiplayer stories that we had in mind. We were going to build high-quality social story games you can play with friends in the length of a movie. Velvet Sundown is the first game of the genre: a story taking place in a luxury yacht where it's hard to tell a friend from a foe.

Our original plan was to complete the game in the six months we had. Our runway ended at six months, so we had to timebox the project. We even ordered a roll-up banner that said, "Velvet Sundown – coming summer 2011." I think we still have that banner somewhere—it's kind of funny and brings back memories.

We kept building and showing the first versions (with almost no gameplay) to people and talking about it. We got some encouraging feedback and tuned our pitch according to the reactions we got. We realized very quickly that there was probably a good reason why "multiplayer stories" were not common—they are extremely complex to build. From the start, we had to create our own technology to develop the stories.

We were also fast running out of months, which equaled money. I had to raise another round. I had been pitching at events, but there wasn't much money moving in the angel scenes in Finland, and I didn't have the connections—I had to build them.

Finally, we found an angel fund that was willing to invest 100,000 euros in us. We had several meetings with them, and it took around two months to go through—which should have been faster. After we had agreed on the valuation, they sent us the terms that suddenly included the fund receiving options as well! I talked to our advisors to see if this was normal. It was not normal, but a way for the other party to haggle the already agreed valuation. I got mixed advice: some said run fast; others said that if there was money on the table, grab it. We continued negotiations and finally ended with terms that suited both parties. Then came the time to sign—at which point we heard they couldn't go forward. They didn't actually have the cash, and the bank had said "No" to a loan going towards a startup investment. It was a bad time to cash in on their stocks, and selling real estate was too slow. So basically, they never had the money to invest that we'd been negotiating for. That was a "back to the drawing board" moment after a lot of time lost.

Our second round was finally raised just after Midsummer (a national celebration in June) and mostly from family and friends—but this time, more friends joined. Tekes also continued to support us with a second project.

In July 2011, we finally had our first properly playable build. We played it at the office, and it was great fun. Of course, you could say we were biased, but I still remember the exhilaration after playing and the mental relief—it actually works!

Closed Beta at Arctic 15

But you don't really have a business if you're the only one playing your games, so we pressed forward. I applied – and was accepted – to pitch as one of the fifteen companies in Arctic15 that was held in the autumn of 2011. We only had like three months to finalize a game that we could actually launch.

Games always have a ridiculous amount of "polish" you need to do when the core game already works – you need all kinds of menus and features and graphics to make the experience accessible. With our crew of six founders, we never even really got to the "polish" phase. We did the bare minimum or MVP as it's commonly called.

The Arctic15 pitch went well – I practiced by heart every word of the 15-minute pitch that I had. That's my way of pitching: lots of practice so I'm confident I know what I'm saying, that I no longer feel scared standing there, and it frees me up to improvise. A little bit of excitement is good, but not too much.

Arctic15 also started our first "closed beta" phase where users with the code could come and play the game. We started to get real users for the game!

Soft Launch for the Webgame

After the mad dash to be able to release a closed beta, we looked at the feedback we were getting and a lot of it was something we already knew we should do. We had to improve the matchmaking/lobby system of our multiplayer game and we needed more content. The problem was that multiplayer stories were very complex – and we were too slow to build them. We'd have to improve that cycle. It would not make sense to improve that cycle when we could – more easily for us – improve that cycle by improving the tech. However, money was again short and we needed more time.

We got some connections from Arctic15, but more than that my own network had grown in the past year and I started to know where to look for the right connections. That was the time I met the CEO of an accounting company who had much knowledge and connections in the Finnish tech startup scene. His support and connections were an invaluable part of us raising our third and biggest angel round of 200,000 euros.

That enabled us to do the necessary development to get the Velvet Sundown game properly launched. During the winter of 2011-2012, we also renamed the underlying technology to Dramagame, for which it is still known. At this point, we also started to think whether this development may have led to something patentable. We found a super patent attorney who, from a couple of meetings with us, could deduce the patentable core and write that down into a patent like she had been there from the beginning building it with us. (The patent was later granted after a long process in 2015.)

In summer 2012 we first relaunched the closed beta and then soft-launched it to the public. This was 1.5 years after we had started the development of Dramagame: Velvet Sundown.

At this point, Velvet Sundown was a 3D webgame. You would have to install a browser plugin to play, but that was not the reason we failed to attract enough users. The high time of webgames had just passed and the iPad was taking over.

We had discussed before if we should go iPad first, but for many good reasons we didn't. We were doing a new type of gameplay and we needed to playtest on real users: Appstores are not very good for allowing early unpolished trials to get into distribution. We were also encouraged by very reputable advisors to go with flash technology first, and that in retrospect would've been a bad choice, which exemplifies that it is only in retrospect easy to say what should've been done.

So we had a webgame available for PC. We got really good feedback on the game and how it "brings a whole new level to storytelling," but business-wise things did not add up. We had to think of something else.

2. STRATEGY: LICENSING TECHNOLOGY AND BUSINESS GAMES

Over the summer of 2012, while we were launching our webgame, we had also applied for our third project with Tekes. This time, it was as part of a consortium of companies building media-related cloud technologies. The project was not very big (less than 100,000 euros) but required private funding, which we got through a crowd-funded stock sale. We sold B-stock (without a voting right) through a company that handled the actual selling for us, and I have to say that was the easiest ever funding round from the entrepreneur's perspective. This company had started operations just recently, and we were one of their two first customers. The round closed in August. Unfortunately, at that time, the biggest sum you could crowd-sell your stock for was 100,000 euros. Later on, the company went on to raise rounds in the millions, but for us at the time, it would not have been an option.

Altogame

Later in the autumn of 2012, we went to pitch at yet another pitching competition that was also a part of a media conference. Ville-Kalle and I were traveling with our couple-of-months-old baby, and our son was with the grandparents.

The pitch went well but didn't win the judges. We disagreed with the judges on who should've won but somehow agreed it was not for us. We didn't have enough momentum going. We still had some money, but we needed more air under our wings.

At a restaurant after the conference, we had a serious talk together about where we should be going. It was obvious we had good technology but equally obvious the game as such was not flying. We decided we'd have to maximize benefits from the tech one way or another.

We were already in talks with the founders of Altonova, who later changed their name to Altogame. The founders are a Finnish couple with all kinds of Ph.D. and book-publishing credentials who were bringing methods from music performer coaching to business.

Before Christmas, we made a deal with them to create a game. The game IP would be theirs, we would do the development, and the game would license our technology base.

The match of our talent and theirs was a very good one, and we ended up creating two very widely applicable business titles: Lateral Gallery (published 2013) and Agile Avenue (published 2014). The Altogame has lived on longer than Tribe Studios on its own momentum. The company later moved to London.

Young Innovative Companies

Altogame made us have an actual platform technology that supported multiple titles. Now we were able to apply a new strategy for our business: making serious games for learning and other useful purposes.

We quickly gathered a pipeline of interested partners and made new sales materials to attract momentum. In spring 2013, we also applied to Tekes Young Innovative Companies program, which was their best startup program, giving a sizable 70% of funding as a grant.

The spring of 2013 was a hectic time, and I have only sparse memories. I was pitching for a new round of private funding, I was pitching to potential customers to make sales, and we were building a new game. This was all under the new B2B strategy of working with partners to create games. We also got on board a well-connected advisor/sales agent in Silicon Valley. All the while switching the caretaking activities of our 6m+ old child with the dad.

One extra missed heartbeat came right in January 2013 in the form of a sizable bill from our work pension provider. These are mandatory payments in Finland that can be paid in yearly or monthly tracking. We were on the monthly tracking plan but somehow, as a combination of the new accounting company, new executive assistant, and an old me getting a baby, none of us noticed we'd missed payments on this in the past year. The bill was altogether around 50,000 euros. That was a lot, because as it happens, we only had about ~50,000 euros in our bank account, and salaries for nine people were due in two weeks. Our accounting company totally handled the negotiations for a payment schedule to be organized, and it took us long into the year to get it all paid.

Tip for politicians:
Make employment side costs simple to handle!

Currently the employment side costs in Finland vary between 20-25% of the employee's salary. So that if the employee gets 1000 euros the company has to pay 200 – 250 euros extra to the government in various fees.

These various fees are calculated in many different ways and can be very hard to keep up with. I've never even tried to get the details of it and have always had an accounting company to handle them. Even then though, mistakes can happen, as is highlighted in the story above. Much better would be to say it's a fixed tax rate, e.g. 22% that is paid always together with the salary that you pay. So that it would be one single fee paid to a single governmental organization. Would make life of an entrepreneur a lot easier!

I remember the day when I first heard about that bill. I had trouble concentrating on other things later on the day because I was trying to rationalize my mind around the thought "it's ok, we'll get it paid". When we left the office with Ville-Kalle he was ranting about something production related. How this or that should be different. I judged it to be a bad time to talk about missing 50k euros in pension payments so I kept the information to myself for some days longer until the payment timeline was negotiated. That action of not telling something bad instantly is something I call "shielding" and that's what a startup CEO/founder is doing every now and then towards the team. You shield them from the bad news. You figure out a basic survival strategy first and then go out with the information. If everyone was experiencing every note of the depths of the valleys it would be too disruptive. I'm sure it worked the other way around too and our technical founders didn't bother me with the technical crisis before they had also a plan to present.

But then, back to the funding in the spring 2013. The Young Innovative Companies funding application included a pitch to a VC jury who would judge if the case was interesting. We got a greenlight from them and subsequently in June Tekes gave us a greenlight for their 250 000 euros grant provided we got 100 000 euros of private money by the end of August. That greenlight from Tekes was not the only good thing that happened in June. We also secured up to 225 000 of project-based funding for making a new version of the original Velvet Sundown game. This funding would be paid back in royalties from the income of the game and would be used to develop the game to a new downloadable format with more and better content.

So we could have a semi-restful entrepreneurial summer vacation in the July. I had this nagging feeling though that I did not have enough funding yet to make it to 100 000 euros so I did keep working on that as much as the business angels were reachable over summer. One of the deals got closed over phone when I was at the top of a tundra hill in the Finnish Lapland with our family.

Come August though we were still missing 55 000 euros and the deadline was approaching fast. It felt nauseating that the government was ready to hand-over 250 000 euros if only the angels would back that up with a 100 000 euro bill. This round was somehow the hardest mentally, perhaps because we had so good momentum on many scales that it felt strange we would not find backing now when we had found it previously. Also it was increasingly hard to find time to sell the product when the selling of the stock was dragging along so long.

Then I got a call from a potential business partner with whom we had discussed we might do co-operation after this YIC round was closed. They said they had thought about it and they would go ahead and fund us to get that round closed. This was in fact the start of them later creating an angel fund that is one of the more active funds in Finland and that organizes regular highly educational events for entrepreneurs.

But back to the call. I was mesmerized. Could this be the ticket I was so much waiting for? I remember it was a long call and during that I kept drawing lines and shapes to our office whiteboard. At the end the board was a mess of colors zigzagging everywhere. I kind of wish I had taken a photo before wiping it. That deal was closed quickly in about one week which left us almost a week to the deadline set by Tekes. We were again ready to conquer the world.

More partners, more games

During the fundraising the team had been already working for the second version of Velvet Sundown, which was kind of a separate strand, but also much related. Altogame's first problem-solving game Lateral Gallery launched in the autumn.

We worked heavily to find more companies to partner for Dramagame products. And soon we signed up two new partners in Finland and hired a person to help with the sales too. I flew to Silicon Valley three times that year and got several big international partners lined up for potential sales.

One big case came from an educational conference held in London in early 2014. We made a paid proof-of-concept game for them during the spring. This was one of those deals that could make a startup. We were talking about a >1million UK pound contract to create a series of online learning games with Dramagame. Unfortunately this was not the one for us and in the end the partner opted for a more traditional type of eLearning. It came very close though.

Time flies quickly and we soon learned by experiencing it, that 6-12 months is a normal lead time in B2B sales. Especially so in Finland when the country was suffering from a downturn and companies were rather cutting from extra investments than thinking about improving processes with technology.

We were also selling a whole new type of product, so we had to learn the right process for selling it. Like in the beginning we were lacking an easy demo game we could experience with any customer by taking a maximum of ten minutes out of a meeting for that. Later, we created "the Closing Game", a small scenario designed for sales training.

Big time investors found our model too complex. We had a technology that we were licensing, but at the same time our lineup of partners was not able to build the products themselves. So at the same time we had a service business where the partner could order the game development from us. This led us to experiment with a third strategy.

3. STRATEGY: MIDDLEWARE COMPANY

In the spring of 2014, we assembled the idea of becoming a purely middleware company. We would only be building technology for others to license. Essentially, the others would have to be game companies at the start to be able to use the technology. We had received some inbound requests regarding this and wanted to test the idea.

How we actually ended up testing this approach was at the upstairs coffee shop at Victoria Station in London. That was the place where we met a partner of a VC firm who was very knowledgeable about the gaming industry. Ville-Kalle and I pitched him the idea of making Dramagame into a licensable game engine.

We had done the calculations on how many game companies we would need using it, how the pricing would work, etc., but it was essentially all just on paper. The team was working on creating games for existing partners, and no one had actually started to work towards a fully licensable codebase. That would have required certain actions to improve the interfaces to functionalities.

However, that single meeting with the VC in London was enough to convince us this was not the right strategy for us.

He had very convincing knowledge about the history of other game engines and how it is a long struggle to reach the top. And the top is where you need to be to make it at all as a game engine provider.

We were a little bit downcast after the meeting but very thankful still. It had saved us a lot of time and hassle going down a path we could not afford and would not have been funded for. If this guy wouldn't buy the idea, then anyone who did probably wouldn't know what they were doing.

4. STRATEGY: DOWNLOADABLE GAME

So we were struggling to turn the business profitable with our licensing business. In the meantime, we had switched the product itself from only a web-based technology into a downloadable application. For our Velvet Sundown game, this meant we could embed it into some of the most successful online game stores.

At the time, Steam was, and still is at the time of writing, the most successful and biggest online game store. Steam had a Greenlight process where you had to pitch your game idea, and the community would vote on which ones got into the store.

We had sent Velvet Sundown into Steam Greenlight a long time ago, and it was getting a lot of both upvotes and downvotes, so it was not moving in the charts. In fact, the game spent more than a year in the process. We found that the most active Steam community was not easy to win over with our Dramagame ideology.

The new launch time was nearing in spring 2014, and we had to increase visibility and our efforts. We hired a PR office that organized many beta players for us by distributing beta codes through various sites. At the same time, we got connected to a Steam Account Manager who was very favorable to having our game in the store.

While the negotiation on including our game was successful, the closed beta itself raised our visibility, and the upvotes started to win over the downvotes. Officially, in June 2014, the community voted us through Greenlight.

Velvet Sundown launched on Steam in July 2014. Somehow many of our launches and fundraising activities always happened over summer. That is a difficult time in the Nordic countries to attract attention because the countries mainly shut down for summer vacations in July. However, games are global products, and the same does not apply globally.

The Steam store worked very well for us, and we gained many fans through the service. We had feared this might not be the case, knowing that Steam is better known for more hardcore gaming titles. It was great to see our game finally get players' interest on a bigger scale.

The press we got was also very good. In the six months following the launch, we were covered in most of the big and small gaming press: Edge, VentureBeat, GamesIndustry.biz, Gamasutra, Gamesauce, Kotaku, Killscreen, PC Gamer, Pelaaja, Polygon, RockPaperShotgun, and others.

We also got into the finals of gaming awards organized by Game Connection. We went to that conference and came back with a trophy for the "Best European Social Game."

But we were not making money. The free-to-play model had worked to educate the player base, but monetization was not working at all. Due to contractual reasons, it was impossible to raise more funds to work on that, and we were again really, really low on funds.

At the same conference where we won the trophy, there was also one meeting that took place that led us to rethink our game…

5. STRATEGY: CHAT GAME

At the Paris Game Connection 2014, an Asian company wanted to meet us. In these kinds of industry conferences, you get many requests for meetings from service providers—companies that help you acquire users, expand geographically, create graphics, localize your games, etc. I tend to be selective about meetings to ensure relevance and potential for cooperation or deals. This Asian company didn't meet my usual criteria, but they were listed on the stock exchange, so I thought it might be interesting.

The company had a popular chat application on the market. Among many things we discussed, the representative mentioned that our gameplay style would be interesting for them, even though they weren't currently doing anything like it. It was a small remark that could've easily been dismissed as a random suggestion. Happily, Ville-Kalle was sitting in the meeting with me, and the idea stuck with him.

We had previously considered a tablet strategy to bring our 3D graphics-based games to iOS and Android. However, we hadn't dreamed of going mobile because of the typing required to play our games. All Dramagames rely heavily on conversation, where players discuss with each other to solve missions or quests. Mobile games usually favor simple interfaces like one-button or swipe controls, so introducing a multiplayer game with heavy typing seemed impractical.

But here was the breakthrough. When we refined the idea, we realized we could—and should—pivot to chat apps. Messaging platforms like WhatsApp, Facebook Messenger, WeChat, Line, Tango, Kakao, Snapchat, Viber, and others had risen in prominence since we started in 2010. The opportunity felt so obvious that we wondered why we hadn't thought of it earlier.

Finally, we had a mobile strategy. Pitching to investors anything that wasn't mobile had always been difficult. While "investability" isn't the ultimate measure of success, it's still a strong signal of the times. This strategy aligned everything for us, but we were utterly out of money. We had not paid salaries to ourselves for a long time. We only covered two employees regularly, along with other company expenses.

One evening in November 2014, I stayed late at the office and called through all our existing investors. I explained our dire situation. By the end of that evening and with three new angels joining, we raised our fifth angel round, totaling about 80,000 euros.

One reason we urgently needed funds was a trip to Shanghai. A month earlier, Ville-Kalle and I had met with a highly influential business associate who could help us penetrate the Chinese market and secure investments. I made the trip, and although it didn't lead to a groundbreaking deal, it very well could have.

Overall it took a month to turn the ship and make the pivot. This was basically the time when Ville-Kalle sold the idea to everyone in the team. By January 1, 2015, all other activities stopped. No more work on Velvet Sundown or new B2B partner sales. Everyone—all seven of us—was focused on the Dramagame on chat app strategy. We refined our presentations and started building a prototype to sell to a chat app publishing partner.

In late 2014, VC discussions were going better than ever, and we reached out to five chat apps for potential publishing. All of them were interested in seeing our demo. However, we were still short on funds, and every week counted. In February 2015, we were accepted to a promising startup pitching event in San Francisco. I had to secure flights, but my company and personal credit cards were maxed out. Thankfully, our travel agency extended credit until a B2B payment came through, and I made the trip, gaining a new card to play.

Before that trip and amidst all the fundraising, a new possibility had already emerged. In January, at a mobile gaming conference in London, we met with a local chat application company called Palringo. We suggested the idea of creating a game for them to publish. They already had group games in their service, and it seemed like a natural fit. When Tiki, Ville-Kalle and myself went to meet with Tim Rea, Palringo's CEO, in the lobby of a hotel, it quickly became evident that we had mutual interests. Tim made it clear he wasn't interested in a publishing partnership, but he saw real potential in acquiring our company.

While the acquisition was being discussed, we also received a funding offer from a US-based fund I had met during my trip. They were ready to invest $200,000 immediately in our strategy of building multiplayer story games inside messaging apps. It was very tempting, but compared to the acquisition, the amount simply wasn't enough. We would have needed more to fully support the pivot and build this new market. At the time, no messaging platform—except Palringo—had yet integrated games into their chat apps.

Everything moved quickly with the acquisition. Within two months, we agreed on the deal's baseline, and Palringo began subcontracting all Tribe Studios work while finalizing the remaining details. None too soon—our accounting company had just threatened to halt services due to overdue payments. I assured them everything would be covered the following week.

During the Palringo subcontracting period, it hit me just how much we had been relying on sheer willpower over the past 12 months. "Willpower" was a term Ville-Kalle and I often used, borrowed from roleplaying games where characters have an extra trait called “willpower.” If you roll the dice badly, you can “burn” one willpower to try again, and over time, the willpower would regenerate. In tight spots, Ville-Kalle and I would joke, “Let’s burn one willpower,” and then press on as if nothing had happened. We had been burning through it for a year.

That subcontracting period was grueling, as I had learned by then that a deal isn’t a deal until it’s signed. At that point, I was deeply relieved by the prospect of selling the company, as the idea of returning to the uncertainty and risks of fundraising was far from appealing.

Fortunately, everything was finalized, and in May 2015, the papers were signed. Overnight, we leapt into a whole new league of startups. We transitioned from struggling with revenue to being revenue-positive, and from a small fanbase to a large one, gaining significant momentum in many ways.

All seven team members, our patented technology, and our collectively regenerating willpower transferred from Tribe Studios Oy to Palringo Finland Oy, marking the start of an exciting new chapter.

PART II ADVANCED MATERIAL

Dear Diary,

Today it is reality. I feel good as I look at the mounting number of likes appearing in Facebook and other channels. I've just posted the news of our exit. The likes feel good like we're all conditioned to feel warm about other people noticing what we're up to and liking that. However, in the whole process, this seems just one of those emotional highs that I've been getting. The truth is I've been processing the exit already for weeks and I feel different.

Yesterday I happened to glimpse in a mirror on our kitchen wall. I was a bit startled that I still look the same. I look just like I did only a couple of months back when there was yet no certainty of our exit. But the emotional state I'm in right now is something different. I've been processing the event for weeks already and I'm still not done.

Tribe Studios started officially in Autumn 2010. I had started the planning phases already six months before. That makes it exactly five years from the start now. It is five years of running a startup and the total commitment that comes with that. It has been a ride.

Unfortunately, I have not exactly kept a diary. That would make this easy. I could just take my pages and publish them. Now I have to rely on my memories and random notes along the way. But why should it be easy? What would be the challenge there?

Elina

1. "THE ONLY THING HE LACKED WAS INEXPERIENCE" (ABOUT TEAM)

Dear Diary,

Today was the first day of my startup journey, although I didn't really know it for sure yet. With a group of colleagues from the gaming industry, we gathered around our kitchen table to discuss founding our own company. Naturally, we also warmed up the sauna to continue the talks. This didn't turn out to be the last time we talked. Later, we also met at our summer cottage, and finally, on a sunny day in July 2010, filed the papers for Tribe Studios. The official founding date became 21st of August.

Elina

"Culture Eats Strategy for Breakfast"

Everyone keeps saying the team is important for a startup, and I agree. A successful startup needs people who are not only good at what they are doing but also have an inner motivation to excel.

There are many theories about the perfect team, but there is no one-size-fits-all model. I remember listening to a talk by Mårten Mickos in the early days at the Slush conference we participated in 2010. Back then, Slush was still a relatively small event. We had just won the Startup Sauna accelerator, so I was pitching at the finals too! I remember my slides didn't work, and I only noticed halfway through the pitch but didn't miss a beat. Mårten said two things that stuck with me: "Don't over-engineer your team. There is always a component of 'this happened to be the people we did it with.'" The other phrase was, "The only thing he lacked was inexperience," referring to an experienced CEO who lacked the fresh perspective of seeing things for the first time. Essentially, he was saying it's okay to be a first-time CEO and that it could even be advantageous in some situations.

We ended up doing okay with our technically excellent but startup-wise inexperienced team. Intuitively, we realized we needed to get the company culture right from the outset. In the beginning, we spent much more time talking about how to run the company than what our product would actually be.

We wanted to create a motivating environment for top experts—people who genuinely know what they do and don't like being micromanaged. Heikki had recently read Drive by Daniel H. Pink, which validated that motivation comes from "Autonomy, Mastery, and Purpose." Autonomy means control over your working methods. Mastery means the ability to develop skills. Purpose means understanding why you're doing something and feeling it has significance. Notably, the list does not include "Money." While money is necessary and should be sufficient to cover your basic needs, it does not foster the kind of intrinsic motivation essential for effective and meaningful work.

Another ideology we borrowed from was ROWE—Results Only Work Environment by Cali Ressler and Jody

Thompson. The tagline goes, "Everyone is free to work whenever and wherever they like as long as the job gets done." This requires meaningful goals and not just sitting in an assigned chair from 9 to 5.

These cultural ideologies may seem self-evident to many working in knowledge-based jobs, but they are surprisingly revolutionary and demanding to implement. One notable challenge we encountered was that running ROWE can go against Finnish Trade Union Treaties. Finnish companies are required to closely monitor employees' working hours to prevent unpaid overtime, which complicates implementing flexible work policies. While this wasn't an issue for our core team of startup founders—who aren't covered by such protections—it became an important consideration when hiring additional employees.

TIP for politicians:
Allow flexible time for work. We are no longer slaves to factory lines.

Another issue was self-leadership. In a startup, everyone must lead themselves, but some people struggled with this. High expectations and a lack of middle management meant we couldn't keep employees who needed more guidance, even if their work skills were good.

Throughout Tribe's history, we maintained a flat organization and never grew beyond ten people. It took us some time to understand what working at Tribe Studios was truly like: a highly rewarding and motivating environment, but also very demanding for anyone not already confident in their skills. This meant we could only hire top-tier, AAA-level talent—a far more challenging task than we initially anticipated. However, with time, we learned how to navigate this.

The biggest lesson? Never take hiring lightly. It requires

rounds of interviews, recommendation checks, and patience. But motivation and attitude can outweigh pure technical skill. We found AAA talent among both new graduates and industry veterans.

"The Only Place Where Greatness Comes Before Hustle Is in the Dictionary"

So, what was my role in the startup? What does a startup CEO do? A great founding team is often said to consist of three roles: the hustler, the designer, and the coder. The CEO is typically the hustler, responsible for fundraising, selling, marketing, networking, business development, hiring, and contracts.

In my case, I shared much of the hustling with my co-founder husband. I handled day-to-day hustling like pitching, sales meetings, and organization, while he constantly generated ideas and tested our vision: "How about we combine this with that?"

Overall, I enjoyed hustling, although the two most challenging aspects were raising money and managing focus. More on these in the next chapters.

"Don't over-engineer your team."

Our founding team was six people at the start, and it included a married couple—that was like two red flags! It worked for us, and I don't think there was any other way we could have succeeded.

When I was out pitching the startup, I was often asked, "How did you get such an experienced team?" The answer, of course, was that we were all co-founders.

There was no way we could have raised enough money to truly compete with market-level salaries for the founders. And the talent was needed: what we were building was a very demanding gaming product. It was probably a bit crazy to even attempt that with six people.

Two people left before the exit, but it wasn't a problem since we had a solid shareholders' agreement in place for situations like that. Timo left to found Zorg Entertainment, and Jarkko became a founder at PlayRaven. HC joined later with co-founder status, so at the time of the acquisition, we had five co-founders.

2. "ABR – ALWAYS BE RAISING" (ABOUT MONEY)

Dear Diary,

Today money was short. I did not pay myself a salary last month, and I'm not quite sure if I will next month. I have no idea when the next money will hit my bank account. However, I was called to get interviewed on a morning TV show tomorrow. It's the Finnish national TV, and I'll be talking about entrepreneurship. We are one of the finalists of the Arctic15 event on the same day. The crowd at the event is smaller than the broadcast TV audience, but I should be equally presentable. I have nothing to wear, as I haven't purchased new clothes for about a year. Luckily, my credit card still has balance!

Elina

Getting Investment

Okay, if it wasn't obvious before, this is where you see we are not in Silicon Valley but Europe. Every now and then, you hear somebody proclaiming in Talouselämä (the Finnish economic weekly magazine) that there is plenty of risk money in Finland but a lack of good targets. That is simply not true. You never hear that from someone who's actually run a startup and tried to raise money for it. Another myth is "Good companies always get invested in." Equally untrue, though it may look that way in hindsight. Most winning software companies have gotten investment at some point—you never hear about the rest.

Sadly, I've seen many good European startups fight for years to get funding and only reach meager success, while well-backed Valley startups race to the pole position. The biggest difference is the sheer amount of risk capital available in Silicon Valley. It's not about the know-how of the entrepreneurs—you can read the same blogs—and it's not about Europeans lacking a risk-taking attitude.

Supercell raised more money in its first six months without any product on the market than we did in the total five-year lifetime of Tribe Studios. Of course, money wasn't the only reason for Supercell's super success, but did it give them better odds? Of course, it did.

You can't look at an underfunded startup struggling after 2-4 years and think, "I'm glad I didn't invest in them. They never got anywhere!" The truth is, they might have if they had enough runway to develop clarity in their strategy. When your average runway is 2-3 months, it's hard to think long-term. I know; I've been there. You still do it—you fake like you have six months and decide to worry about money another day. But it's not easy.

DEFINITION: RUNWAY

Runway is the amount of time calculated by dividing the money in your bank account by the monthly burn rate. Do not count money agreed upon but not yet received. Until it's in your bank account, it's still imaginary.

Starting costs for software startups are decreasing. Often, it's just a couple of people with laptops getting a prototype out in weeks. Expectations for startups are rising too, and seed/A-round definitions keep shifting.

In Finland, the funding structure for a startup in our time looked like this:

- ~50,000 EUR to get to a prototype (friends, family, or personal savings).
- ~200,000 – 500,000 EUR to make a product and go to market.
- ~1,000,000 – 5,000,000 EUR to scale.

It's possible to go straight to 1M EUR, but your team needs exits or successes under their belt. The most difficult round is the middle one, 200k – 500k EUR. Finnish angel investors often invest only 5,000 – 10,000 EUR/startup/round, meaning you need a lot of backers. Usually, you end up having multiple rounds. In fact, you are always looking to raise the next round.

Although that is not what the chapter heading is referring to. It is a joke that refers to ABC – Always Be Closing – the salesperson's mantra. ABR means that a startup should always be looking out for opportunities to raise money. The best time to raise money is when you don't need it. The problem with Finnish startups is that they always need money, so by definition, it's never a good time to raise it.

LIST: Top 6 Reasons Not to Invest

1. I don't have money

This is the most common and realistic reason why Finnish business angels don't invest. Many have made previous investments but are now essentially out of money to invest and just enjoying the company of startups and other investors.

The problem arises when an investor is not upfront about their lack of funds, causing entrepreneurs to waste valuable time on discussions that lead nowhere. Angels should quickly clarify their position but can still offer mutually beneficial brainstorming sessions if both parties have the time for it.

2. I don't have time

Angel investors often want to dedicate not only money but also time to the startups they fund. This is reasonable since their involvement can help their investment grow. However, time is limited, and angels already committed to a few companies may not have room for more.

From the entrepreneur's perspective, this can be frustrating. If I'm gathering €100,000 from ten investors, I don't necessarily want all of them to contribute ideas or advice—I just need the money. Sometimes I've felt like saying, "Just give me the damn money," but I've managed to restrain myself.

3. I don't invest in games

This applies to any niche. Investors have focus areas, and certain keywords—like "games"—can be immediate red flags. Sometimes it's because they've had bad experiences with that industry in the past; other times, they're unwilling to learn about its nuances, business models, or strategies.

This creates a mismatch between where money is willing to go and where it's needed. For instance, much of Finland's wealth has historically come from traditional industries like paper or metals, while new startups are often internet-based businesses. Bridging this gap between where money is willing to go and where it is needed is a challenge.

4. You're too early / too late for us

Timing is critical in funding. Some angel funds prefer to

invest in very early-stage startups to secure a large equity stake with minimal investment. This means they're only interested in "two guys and a PowerPoint" scenarios, not more developed ventures.

Sometimes, the window can be surprisingly narrow. I've heard feedback like "you're too early," only to hear six months later, "you're too advanced." Additionally, some investors have unrealistic expectations for what they can get with their money. Their invested amount and valuation expectation would put them to a very early stage investment, but they are actually looking for startups with more traction.

5. I don't invest in startups

When you're raising money, you talk about it constantly and everywhere—it's the only way to get introduced to potential investors. Sometimes, these introductions lead you to financial market professionals.

People often think that some person makes a potential investor because they've made a lifelong career in all kinds of investment products and have a bunch of money and they also know more people with money. The premise might be true but usually they would never invest in startups. They want to play the number game that they know. They want annual growth and predictability. The Startup world doesn't play by their rules. The data they request makes no sense.

6. I don't dig your style

This is perhaps the most subjective but also fundamental reason. Angel investing is a lot like dating—you need to find the right match. Engineers tend to fund engineers, businesspeople fund businesspeople, and so on.

As a woman in the tech startup scene, I've noticed that while being female brings exposure, it doesn't necessarily help secure funding. Most investors are men, and while they'd never consciously admit to bias, it may unconsciously affect their decisions.

Style often becomes a rationalization for why an angel invested. For example, after backing a music startup, an investor might say, "I've always been passionate about music." There's nothing wrong with funding your passions, but as an entrepreneur, you must find people who match your style.

Confession of Love

Finland has one of the best public funding instruments available to startups: Tekes—a funding agency for Technology and Innovation. It covers 50-75% of your R&D budget. For example, if you raise €50,000 from private investors, Tekes matches it with a €50,000 grant—non-diluting money, provided you qualify and complete the reporting. You can pay salaries or outsource services with this funding.

Some dislike Tekes for its bureaucracy, but I've found it flexible on changes and far less hassle than chasing equivalent sums from private investors. I've yet to see a better public funding structure elsewhere. Other government funding instruments often focus on consultancy grants, where you're given allowances to hire consultants. While useful in theory, early-stage startups need to explore their market, shape business models, and create new products—tasks best done by the founders themselves. Consultants can't match the founders' enthusiasm or late-night dedication.

That said, consultations can help if timed well. However, Tekes funding often covers both consultancy and salaries, making other options less relevant for startups.

At the time of publication, Tekes had been rebranded as "Business Finland," though its function remained largely the same. In recent years, government policy has increasingly favored loan instruments. While loans can be valuable for established companies looking to scale, early-stage startups rely on equity investments, not debt. They need risk-tolerant capital, not burdensome loans.

There's No Rulebook

Funding is a game of networking: who you know, and how well you know them. When building your network, think long term. Even if a given investor isn't going to fund you right now, they might fund your next round - or your next startup. Or they may move to another VC fund and be able to invest later. You might also meet someone who is a perfect match for their fund, and be able to make a helpful introduction.

Foster relationships and aim to be helpful. When you start acting as a node connecting people, you become a valuable part of your network. You'll find it easier to make new connections as well.

Good connections often come from people like lawyers and accountants—they know who is actually investing right now, since they handle the deals.

Overall, there is no single rulebook for fundraising, and multiple approaches can work. Yes, there literally are rulebooks, but like any advice, take them with a grain of salt and view them through your own lens.

We did equity crowdfunding before it was fashionable or an "accepted" form of funding. We also used agents—people who take 4–5% of the round if they raise it for you. This is often considered a bad deal, as the CEO is expected to lead fundraising, but it depends: who they are, and when you're working with them. It all depends.

The one thing I'd be careful with when it comes to agents is retainers. If they charge a monthly fee to look for investment, it can become costly and they're not incentivized to move as quickly as you need them to.

Being a funding agent in Finland is actually much easier than in Silicon Valley. This is one of the few areas where the US is more regulated, and you need a high level of paperwork to act as a funding agent. In Finland, it can be part of general advisory work for a startup.

Don't compare your funding journey to someone who counts highly influential VCs as friends or relatives. They are playing a different game. Someone who can raise 5 million in a few phone calls isn't in a position to give useful advice to the rest of us. Do the work and keep building your own network.

Personal Runway

The single biggest expense in startups is salaries. Founding teams typically cut their pay to the bare minimum or work without salaries for extended periods. My advice for those in steady jobs considering a startup journey: start saving now. Personal financial preparedness is critical.

Defining your personal runway—the time you can go without a salary—is challenging. Often, you can stretch further than you initially imagine. My husband and I went 12 months without pay at one point. If I'd known at the start that it would take a year, I might have called it quits. But luckily, I didn't know.

Initially, we thought we could manage six months by borrowing money and reevaluating after. Those six months passed, and we'd just launched a product gaining good traction and press. Excitement kept us going. Then came a month where several sales deals closed—not enough to pay ourselves but enough to stay motivated.

Finally, we developed a new strategy—one that led to our exit. The heat was on as we raised a bridge round from current investors and held serious talks with several institutional venture capital funds. Throughout this, stopping never felt like an option, despite having no income.

How did we manage? Honestly, I'm still unsure. We used every bit of savings, sold personal assets, borrowed money, and even relied on grandparents to help with our children's expenses.

Am I glad we did it? Absolutely. Would I do it again? Maybe not. I now appreciate working in a company with a more balanced bottom line and solid institutional backing. I can focus entirely on productive work rather than scrambling for survival funds.

LIST: How You Know Your Startup Is Low on Cash

1. Your financial ledger lists multiple collection agencies as vendors.
2. You delay bills until after payday to prioritize non-founder salaries.
3. You optimize payments based on how quickly each vendor resorts to collections.
4. You regularly check if personal account transfers are needed to cover company expenses.

Being out of money for long stretches also brought unexpected clarity. I could walk through shopping centers without feeling compelled to buy anything. I purchased only what was necessary, avoiding impulse buys altogether. While I've since allowed myself some indulgence, I still try to avoid unnecessary purchases. One thing I don't miss: always choosing the cheapest option. These days, I value quality, whether it's food, clothing, or other essentials. For instance, I'm happy to afford organic produce now, and it feels like a well-earned reward.

3. "DON'T ASK FOR PERMISSION. ASK FOR FORGIVENESS." (ABOUT TIME)

Dear Diary,

We are about six months into our startup and I've just realized I'm dropping stuff. Unintentionally. I'm not planning it, but I just can't keep up. I got invited to speak at an event, but I saw the invite only after the event had passed. Emails are piling up, I'm travelling to conferences and meeting people and I need to follow up, respond, plan, and sell. There are opportunities I might miss because I just didn't have time to pay attention. Acknowledging this is a relief. I have to let go and not try to control everything. I can't be on top of everything. The good news is I only have to be on top of the things that matter. Focus! Focus! Focus!

Elina

Selling

Selling is one of the most important things a startup founder/CEO does. You keep selling the pitch to investors, selling the vision to the team, and selling the product to customers. Ideally, the order should be reversed: first sell to customers, then to the team, and only then to investors. If you've read the investment chapter, you may guess that it's frustratingly easy to spend too much time on fundraising, even when you'd rather be focusing on other types of selling.

Pitch

The 30-second to 1-minute pitch is the startup's most essential tool for selling. It's your opening line: what do you do and why? Why should anyone care?

A structured 5-15 minute pitch is often used for attracting investment when presenting to investors. However, I've found it relatively ineffective for this purpose. It's much better to have a meaningful conversation with investors than to pitch to them from a stage. No matter how good your on-stage pitch is—and mine was often complimented—it rarely opens wallets unless you build a relationship with the people who control the money or their close associates.

Even so, knowing your investment pitch is crucial for several reasons:

1. It clarifies your business. A solid pitch forces you to distill your vision and strategy.
2. It provides valuable feedback. If your audience asks irrelevant or confused questions, your pitch isn't clear enough. If they ask nothing, it might be too complex or uninteresting. Good questions indicate your pitch is resonating and can help you refine your approach.
3. It builds your network. A clear pitch often leads to references like, "Have you talked to X? They might

fund or buy this." These referrals help you identify the right people to meet.

For us, our investment deck and sales deck were always the two most up-to-date descriptions of our business plan.

PR and Media

PR and media are somewhat vanity metrics for startups. It's nice to see your name and face in the paper, but it may not directly advance your business. Ideally, every PR effort should aim to achieve a specific goal. Whose attention are you trying to capture, and why? Are you selling the product, attracting investors or buyers, or perhaps recruiting?

We've always found it relatively easy to get press attention. Being a woman in the tech startup and gaming scenes helps—both industries still have a gender imbalance. Often, event organizers or journalists think, "It'd be great to have a woman here," and I get the call.

It's harder to measure how much this has actually helped. While some excellent connections have come from media exposure, it also generates noise. More people contact or call you, but not all of them contribute meaningfully.

For product marketing, we occasionally used a PR agency and achieved good coverage for our games. However, the conversion rate from PR and blog posts to actual users was underwhelming. Great PR should never be your only user acquisition strategy.

B2B vs. B2C

Startups often struggle with whether to sell to businesses (B2B) or consumers (B2C). We've done both at times.

B2C typically requires more investment because early-stage consumers rarely pay enough to fund further development.

B2B, on the other hand, has long sales cycles (6-12 months in Europe at the time of writing), but you may find an early buyer willing to make a significant purchase, giving you the funds to move forward.

This decision should come from the founders and depend on how you plan to validate your product-market fit. What is the best use case for your product, and what vision are you passionately pursuing?

Travel and Conferences

Global markets demand a global presence. While video calls have improved from the time we started, they can't replace face-to-face networking entirely. That said, it's easy to waste time attending too many irrelevant events.

It's often hard to determine the value of an event until you've attended. Sometimes you need to take a chance. What works for one startup—or even for your own startup at an earlier stage—might not work later.

We quickly outgrew many events. While giving back to the community by advising at events is rewarding, it shouldn't become the norm if your time is better spent elsewhere.

Tips for spotting valuable events:

- Invite-only events (check the credibility of the inviter).
- Events recommended by trusted colleagues with high-caliber attendees.
- Events where you're invited to pitch or speak, as these often provide more value.
- Events with a significant presence of potential customers. Don't just network with other startups—focus on selling to customers.

Email

Email is a beast. Everyone hates it nowadays, and it's likely that email will eventually be replaced by more efficient messaging systems. In China, for instance, business-critical communications are often conducted via chat apps, which are faster, more convenient, and less spammy.

Many strategies exist for managing email chaos. My approach aims for inbox zero. Filters route specific emails directly to subfolders, while I manually move processed emails to an "Email" folder. Quick replies like "OK," "Great," or "Thanks" are sent immediately. For emails requiring a longer response, I add them to my to-do list and move them out of the inbox.

Despite these strategies, my inbox sometimes accumulates messages in a gray area between quick replies and more complex responses. These linger until I set aside time to process them.

LIST: Types of Email You Get

1. Sales Emails
   These come from companies pitching process-enhancing software, conference services, or other offerings. While I sympathize with salespeople—having done B2B sales myself—I rarely engage with these beyond the subject line.
2. News Bulletins
   Startup conferences lead to many business card exchanges, often resulting in subscriptions to founders' email lists. While it's good practice for startups to maintain mailing lists, these can become overwhelming. I unsubscribe from most, except for close friends' updates or something where I'm an actual customer.

3. Questionnaires

   These range from academic studies on startups to annual industry surveys. Every event or product wants your feedback. While some are worthwhile, many feel like a time sink. I answer selectively.

4. Informative Lists

   Industry news bulletins are valuable but can quickly become excessive. I've limited my subscriptions to three: one for startups, one for the gaming industry, and one for transmedia.

5. Job Seekers

   Although we rarely advertised job openings, we received many unsolicited applications. While I tried to respond politely to all, this wasn't always feasible. Occasionally, these emails led to fruitful connections.

6. Person-to-Person Communication

   This is the ideal type of email—actual business discussions where agreements are made, plans are developed, and information is exchanged. Unfortunately, this makes up a small fraction of all emails received. Messaging apps' ability to filter and prioritize contacts may eventually replace email for this purpose.

4. "DO WHAT WORKS" (ABOUT PROCESS)

Dear Diary,

Okay, so now it's about time to note that there is no chapter for the product or the idea. Are they not important? Well, not really, no. I mean yes, you need to have one clear vision, focus, and product idea of what it is you're after. But from then on, it's all improvising. It's the process that matters. The execution of the idea.

There are many ways to describe the process of running a startup. The Lean Startup method seems to be the most recognized. Essentially, it's about testing assumptions early with users and pivoting your business model if it isn't working. When you find the right model and achieve product-market fit, you're ready to grow—users and money should start pouring in.

Elina

Book I Read: The Lean Startup by Eric Ries

Best Quote: "The first problem is the allure of a good plan, a solid strategy, and thorough market research. In earlier eras, these things were indicators of likely success. The overwhelming temptation is to apply them to startups too, but this doesn't work, because startups operate with too much uncertainty. Startups do not yet know who their customer is or what their product should be. As the world becomes more uncertain, it gets harder and harder to predict the future. The old management methods are not up to the task. Planning and forecasting are only accurate when based upon a long, stable operating history and a relatively static environment. Startups have neither."

Due to the rapidly changing strategy of a startup, Silicon Valley investors often advise against writing business plans or revenue projections. They view them as a waste of time. Instead, they recommend focusing on marketing and user acquisition plans and cost forecasts. However, most European investors still ask for a business plan and revenue forecast. As an entrepreneur, you'll need to provide those, but don't get fixated on them. Quickly carve them out, use them for their purpose (e.g., raising funds), and then return to building your business.

Running a startup rarely adheres to any pre-existing model. I once heard an excellent metaphor for this: "Behave like a duck." It means, "Look calm and tranquil on the outside, but underneath you're paddling like crazy."

We made many pivots during our journey, but our core technology—the core product—always stayed more or less the same. This highlights an important aspect of pivots: you don't have to change everything. A pivot might involve changing your customer segment, sales channel, or even just how you describe your product.

Meetings?

We've always worked to minimize the time spent in meetings. We even had a sign on our meeting room door that read:

Are you lonely? Tired of working on your own?
Do you hate making decisions?

HOLD A MEETING!

You can:

- See people
- Show charts
- Feel important
- Point with a stick
- Eat donuts
- Impress your colleagues

All on company time!
MEETINGS: The practical alternative to work.

This was meant to discourage unnecessary meetings. Often, information exchange can be done asynchronously using online tools. We've always maintained company-wide chat channels where people can ask questions and discuss issues. This approach is inclusive for remote workers and less disruptive in open offices. Even when sitting in the same room, we often used chat for communication, allowing others to respond when not immersed in other work.

Managers?

Startups need T-shaped people. This concept describes individuals with deep expertise in one area and a broad understanding of many others. Such people can bring value through their specialization while contributing to the bigger picture.

In a startup, everyone needs enough leadership skills to lead themselves analytically and reflect on their self-management. Early startup structures should remain shallow and flexible.

Without middle management, there's no time for micromanaging. You need people who can take ownership of a domain, devise a plan, and execute it. Of course, these plans must align with the overall company vision and goals. That's why it's crucial for everyone to understand and align with the company's overarching objectives.

5. "THIS IS WHERE MIRACLES HAPPEN" (ABOUT MENTAL STRENGTH)

Dear Diary,

I must confess I have some tendency for OCD. You've probably seen the internet memes about mismatched pencils or misaligned tiles. But I've also read a book on the subject, so I know what it actually means. OCD involves impulsive ideas that compel you to do something—like creating symmetry or countering one action with another—to prevent something bad from happening. My OCD is mild, just an occasional tendency. For instance, if my right foot hits the back of a baby stroller, I feel an urge to do the same with my left foot. Symmetry demands it! What might be unusual is that I can resist these urges. It's annoying that my brain sends these signals, but I'm able to disobey.

Sometimes I wonder which came first: Am I able to resist these compulsions because I'm mentally strong, or have these tendencies trained me to be mentally strong?

Elina

The Comfort Zone

There's a saying: you have your comfort zone, and when you wander far enough beyond it, that's where miracles happen. Startups are a fast lane out of your comfort zone.

Faking and Making It

I once filled out a questionnaire that asked, "Do you feel you have sufficient education and resources to perform in your job?" I couldn't help but laugh. What would be the ideal education or resources for a startup CEO? The truth is, there's no such thing. Everybody's winging it. Some people may have expertise to make certain decisions with more confidence, but in a startup, you're constantly confronted with gut decisions. There's often no way to know which choice is correct. You just go with what feels right because, honestly, nobody else could do it any better.

This is especially true in startups where, by nature, you're not only creating new products but often inventing new business models. "Fake it till you make it" isn't quite accurate. A closer phrase would be, "Keep faking it, and you are making it." It's not really even faking it then – it's doing it. Shaping reality through execution. Passion for the process makes it all happen.

As a clarification I must add I'm not advocating lying here! We've seen too many cases where startups have outright lied to their customers, lied to their investors or generally just mangled the truth in unacceptable ways. This chapter is about your mental capacity to lead the business. By your actions of leadership you are making the reality of the company appear from thin air. Your trust in yourself makes that feat of strength be possible.

The Rollercoaster

The common wisdom is that startups are like rollercoasters—high highs and low lows that alternate rapidly. This is true, but the analogy doesn't capture everything. Sometimes, you're going up and down simultaneously. For example, you might be hiring and expanding while also negotiating the next round of funding, which hasn't been secured yet.

Occasionally, these highs and lows occur in quick succession. I vividly remember one such incident at a high-profile event in London. I was mingling with global brand executives when I got a message from an employee: her salary hadn't arrived, and she urgently needed it. What?! I excused myself and found a quiet spot at the back of the venue. Upon calling our accounting company, I discovered that our account was nearly empty. A large payment I had expected hadn't come through. Salaries hadn't been processed. Panic ensued.

Frantically, I sent emails, made calls, and initiated money transfers—including one from my personal account to the employee who needed it most. Within 15 minutes, the immediate crisis was resolved, apologies made, and I took a moment to breathe. I was ready to go back to the cocktail reception. Except I didn't, I decided to take a moment to calm myself and went to the restroom to pump breast milk for my nine-month-old baby. Maintaining the milk supply was important to me, so I took the time to ensure it continued. But after this, then I went back to the mingling and networking.

After that incident, I made it a habit to check the company's account balance three days before payday. It's a habit that stayed with me for years.

What Exactly Causes the Stress?

As humans, we often stress over trivial things: what to serve at a party, whether our kids have enough hobbies, or when to return a call. We should ask ourselves more often, "Is my life how I want it to be?" And if not, "How would I want it to be?"

Startups tend to generate two main types of anxiety:

1. Money Stress

This comes from insufficient funds to execute your plans. I became so used to monthly financial struggles that it felt normal. Working in a profitable company later was a revelation—bills paid on time, no questions asked.

But money stress has an upside: it teaches discipline and focus. Startups with too much money often overspend. Financial constraints force prioritization. Spending money is always easier than earning it.

2. Fear of Failure

This is the "What will people think of me?" stress. Startups exist in a fame-driven ecosystem. There are revered heroes who've made it big, and everyone admires them and aspires to join their ranks.

The harsh reality, though, is that 9 out of 10 early startups are bound to fail. When you share this fact with a room full of entrepreneurs, everyone feels sorry for the nine others.

Thankfully, the startup ecosystem is increasingly trying to embrace failure. In Finland, we have a national Fail Day, started by the local startup ecosystem. There are also international Fail Conferences and similar initiatives. The idea is to frame failure as proof of effort—evidence that you tried something bold, learned from it, and can now move forward.

However, what should be emphasized more is that it's okay to be a failed startup entrepreneur, even if you never become a successful one. At many Fail Day events, the speakers are usually successful entrepreneurs reflecting on their earlier setbacks. The ethos becomes, "It's okay to fail, as long as you try again and eventually succeed." But what if you don't want to do it again? Or if your next attempt doesn't succeed either?

Running a startup is grueling. I wouldn't judge anyone who chooses not to go through it multiple times, whether their first venture was a failure or a success. In some sense, entrepreneurship "gets into your blood," so repeat ventures are common. Nevertheless, anyone who has run a startup—even for a short time—learns invaluable skills and becomes highly employable. This would be my strongest recommendation to anyone considering starting a business: Go and do it. At worst, your market value as an employee will skyrocket.

Of course, this perspective is somewhat idealistic. In Finland, bankruptcy comes with personal financial consequences—damaged credit ratings and other long-term effects. But getting a well-paid job afterward has become more feasible in today's world, helping you recover.

TIP for Politicians:
Stop Banishing Entrepreneurs for Bankruptcy

Sometimes businesses fail. Even those that establish profitable operations may later falter when their environment changes. Punishing risk-taking discourages innovation and adaptability. Without risk-takers, many viable companies might shut down prematurely at the first sign of trouble.

When entrepreneurs try to adapt, there's always a chance their actions won't work, and the business will fail. Bankruptcy is unpleasant for everyone—owners, employees, and customers alike. Entrepreneurs are already excluded from many of the safety nets that regular employees enjoy in Finland, such as sick pay, annual leave, and unemployment benefits. Adding penalties like personal debt and ruined credit ratings is counterproductive.

The consequences can be far-reaching. Having bankruptcy on your record makes you a liability in the eyes of tax authorities when forming a new company. A bad reputation can lead to additional scrutiny, extra checkpoints, and increased bureaucratic costs.

It's often said that entrepreneurs don't fear failure, but that's not true. We do. Nobody likes to fail. Seeing a glowing article about your company's success in a tech blog is far more satisfying than reading one announcing its closure. Questions like, "What will people think of me?" or "Was I not good enough?" can weigh heavily.

For me, I've never cared much about what others think, outside of a small circle. At the heart of that circle is my husband. Since we ran the startup together, we either failed or succeeded as a team, with no need for outside explanations. We'd laugh about the craziness together afterward.

LIST: Ways to Cope with Mental Stress

1. Imagine the Worst
   You build a scenario in your mind of what happens if the worst comes true. For example, when thinking about starting a company, you imagine the worst case: bankruptcy, people laughing at you, someone thinking you were stupid to try, etc. Then you decide whether you can survive that outcome—and if the answer is yes, you go ahead with the risky bet.
2. Boxing Problems
   You mentally place your problem in a box and label it: "To be opened on Monday." For the rest of the week, you don't think about the box or

what it contains. This works, for example, in situations where money is tight and you need to focus on other matters for a while. You can't let financial stress nag at you all the time.

3. 80/20 Rule
   Twenty percent of what you do yields eighty percent of the value. Focus on that 20 percent and let go of the rest. This helps in situations where there is too little time and too much to do - which is almost always the case. The key is to keep evaluating what that 20 percent is. It may not be the same as last week or last month.
4. Shielding
   This is when you don't immediately go to your team to share bad news. Instead, you first develop a plan, or at least the beginning of a way forward, before communicating that a new problem has emerged. It helps if not every low point is shared with equal intensity across the entire team.
5. Tuning Off
   Sometimes you just need to take your mind off work and your startup. This could be sports, walking in nature, or playing with the kids. Let yourself fully immerse in an activity that isn't related to work.

At the beginning of Tribe Studios, I was almost completely immersed in the startup, and the breaks I took were short. I still remember the first night I slept somewhere other than next to my laptop. We went out partying with a friend, and since the grandparents were at home taking care of our son, the plan was to sleep at the friend's apartment so we could truly have the morning off as well.

I remember being out in town when I realized: I didn't have my laptop with me. It had become such an inseparable part of my life that sleeping somewhere without it felt like an event. It's strange to think about it now - probably also a sign of how closely my identity was tied to the company.

"Whether you believe you can or you believe you can't, you are right"

Henry Ford's words resonate deeply. This principle applies not only to startups but to life in general.

What I strive for is not to disconnect too much from what I call "the normal world"—the world of 9-to-5 jobs and clear employer-employee roles. Caring less about others' opinions is very different from becoming thick-skinned and indifferent.

Ultimately, most jobs today require inner motivation and passion. Many people also seek roles that provide purpose beyond just a paycheck. The line between entrepreneur and employee is blurring.

6. "WORK LIKE YOU DON'T NEED THE MONEY. LOVE LIKE YOU'VE NEVER BEEN HURT. DANCE LIKE NOBODY'S WATCHING." (ABOUT WORK-LIFE BALANCE)

Dear Diary,

I just experienced a very intense moment. I used to think I would never work and be with the kids at the same time, but I've had to relax my rule. Situations happen. Like this one. I'm flying off tomorrow for a conference and before I do I need to pay a sizable bill from the company's account. The only problem is I realized I forgot to move the money first from our sibling company to the actual parent company. I'm already home with the kids, and I have the sibling's bank keys at the office. So I call HC, who's still at the office, and with his help, I log on to the online bank and make the transfer. I move on with the kids' evening program, taking the younger one to bath. But the transfer was big, so it requires an extra verification, and the bank calls me. She's asking me to provide the next number on the key card, and I'm telling her I'll just get the card. In reality, I take my laptop and Skype HC to tell me quick what's the next number. So at the same time as I'm calling the bank and Skyping HC with a laptop in my lap, I'm keeping a very close watch on a 1-year-old taking a bath. She sits firmly, but if she decided to get up, she'd be a hazard to herself. Our 5-year-old son is teetering on top of the toilet seat, watching all this unfold.

Elina

Family and a Startup

I've often heard that how families usually cope with the uncertain income of startups is that one person has a steady paid job while the other takes on the startup run. We didn't do this. As mentioned earlier, I was building Tribe with my husband and co-founder, Ville-Kalle, from the start. Ville-Kalle is the imaginative, Da Vinci-type of personality who absorbs information from everywhere around him and combines it into new and fascinating ideas. I'm more of the practical type. I take those ideas and turn them into actionable sequences, PowerPoints, and web content, and I preach them to everyone who needs to know.

We already had a two-year-old son when we started, and our daughter was born two years into building the startup. Finland has very generous policies for parents. The government pays 70% of salary to parents in the following manner: First, the mother has a three-month maternity leave. Then there's a seven-month parental leave, which either parent can take or share, and which grows into eight months if the dad takes the last two weeks of the period. While the mother is on maternity or parental leave, the dad can take a three-week paternity leave, usually right after birth. So basically, for 11 months, one parent gets 70% of their salary covered by the government.

During our daughter's first year, Ville-Kalle and I did a lot of quick hand-offs. She would also come along to the office a lot and take her naps there. She must've thought that the office meeting room was just another extension of our living room. By the time she started moving around faster at six months, we stopped bringing her—it wasn't safe with all the electric cords and equipment.

Sharing everything has been a strength. There are no explanations needed for "How was your day?" Usually, you already know if something was good or bad, and you share the feeling immediately.

Kids naturally bring balance to life. You absolutely cannot work 12-hour days when you have kids—so you don't. You learn to prioritize and work smarter. My procrastination time at work or home is close to zero. I just get to the point. If I sit down at my laptop, I'll write that press release. If I have five minutes, I'll start on the dishes right away.

Sleep and Exercise

Sleep is important. Too little sleep is deadly. During my startup journey, I've sadly heard of several startup founders who passed away unexpectedly. These tragic events leave families behind and often come with no warning. It's hard to pinpoint exact causes, but stress and sleep deprivation likely play a role.

Did I risk my own health during the startup years? At times, probably. My body was often pushed to its limits. My stress tolerance is high, to the point that I rarely feel stressed, or if I do, I can rationalize myself out of it. For example, I'll think, "Right now, at the grocery store, there's nothing I can do about problem X, so there's no reason to stress about it here." I channel stress into action items and tackle them when

I'm in the right place to act.

There were moments, though, when I felt my heart racing too fast. Those moments were wake-up calls—literally—and got me to quickly learn deep breathing to calm myself down. They reminded me of what truly matters in life and helped me regain perspective.

When it comes to sleep, I've always been good at falling asleep quickly. It takes me mere seconds, and I've only had a handful of sleepless nights in years. I can also sleep anywhere; it's like a superpower. I can sleep on planes, trains, boats, the meeting room sofa, or in the car. I especially used to take these car naps when the baby was sleeping in the backseat and we stopped for groceries. Ville-Kalle would do the shopping with our son while the baby and I napped in the car.

Still, I'd often allocate too little time for sleep. At one point, I started tracking my sleep and realized that, over three weeks, the longest night's sleep I'd had was just six hours. That was a wake-up call to make changes. On the bright side, I've always maintained a good level of daily exercise, like walking to daycare and work. This kind of natural activity is great for health.

One particularly active routine was when my kids were one and five years old. They attended different daycare places: the younger one with a nanny with three other children and the older in a larger group. The places were about 1.5 kilometers (one mile) apart, and every morning and afternoon, I ran a triangle between our home and the two places. Without the running, the whole process would have taken an hour; this way, I shortened it to 30 minutes and got some excellent exercise.

Own Time

It's trendy these days to insist on having "your own time." Personally, I haven't had much of it in years while building Tribe. When our daughter was seven or eight months old, I decided to reclaim a small bit of time for myself. From then on, I promised myself that when nature called, I'd go straight to the bathroom, no matter what. Whether the baby was crying, I missed a train, or I was late for a meeting, I'd prioritize this basic need. Surprisingly, this small change significantly improved my quality of life.

But honestly, I don't miss having "me time." I have a dream family and a dream job. What more could I need? Every waking moment feels meaningful. Would it be more fulfilling to spend an hour doing sports than finishing an investment deck? Or to practice an instrument instead of dancing with my kids? For me, the answer is clear.

Of course, I sometimes see friends, play games, or watch TV series with my husband. But even our rare nights out are usually startup parties or industry networking events. It's just the life we've chosen, and I wouldn't trade it for anything.

AFTERWORD: SUCCESS

Somebody asked me once: "Do you consider yourself successful?" This got me thinking, and yes, the answer is yes. But what then does success mean? For me, it's the inner state I'm feeling, that I no longer have to struggle to be accepted by myself. I know what I can do, and I know my strengths. No matter how cliché it sounds, I feel like I walked through fire and survived.

The other ending for this story could've been that I had done a bankruptcy. It was too close too many times for me not to know it was a clear possibility. I would've still had 90% of the learnings I have now. For my personal finances, it would've probably taken 2-3 years to bounce back to the levels they were at before founding Tribe Studios. In that case, it would've been harder for me to consider myself successful. The mental state and amazing experiences would've been 90% there, but we're so used to measuring our lives in money that if the finances went negative, could there have been any success attached to it? I probably wouldn't have written this book either. Would I have been happy with my choice to do the startup? I definitely would have.

The past five years I've enjoyed my life and the thriller. I've always felt like I'm living my life to the fullest. There could not have been anything more that I should or could have been doing. I didn't feel like I was underperforming myself. This is one of the worst fears of our time: What if life goes by without me ever doing anything interesting or meaningful or something that made me feel alive? I haven't had that fear for a long time. And with all I've seen and the energy I still have, I don't feel like I will be standing still anytime soon, whatever I end up doing.

ACKNOWLEDGEMENTS

My deepest gratitude goes to the following people who made this journey possible.

Co-founders

The incredible team that made Tribe Studios.

- Ville-Kalle “Vk” Arponen, CCO, founder from the beginning to end. Also, my other half, husband and soulmate. Your unwavering support, creativity, and partnership have been the foundation of everything.
- Jarkko Kainulainen, Art Director, founder from the beginning to 2013
- Timo “Tiki” Kämäräinen, CTO, founder from the beginning to the end
- Timo Saarinen, Graphics Technology Director, founder from the beginning to 2012
- Heikki Vehmas, Technical Art Director, founder from the beginning to the end
- Jaakko “HC” Väyrynen, Technology Director, founder from 2013 to the end

Family

Our Parents: For always supporting our entrepreneurial journey, often financially and physically, by caring for our kids when we traveled to Silicon Valley, London, Austin, and beyond. In alphabetical order:

- Arja Arponen
- Matti Arponen
- Kari Partanen
- Ritva Partanen

My Wonderful Children, Amos and Ava: You've grown into such marvelous, wondrous people. I can't help but feel that my work and travel did not take away from your upbringing, you've enriched our lives immeasurably.

Advisors, Investors, and Partners

- Ville "Wili" Miettinen, our advisor and investor from the beginning to the end. Your guidance, time, and belief in us made a world of difference, even as you balanced your own business ventures.
- Eija and Olli-Pekka Mäkirintala, from Altogame, who joined us for a significant part of the journey.
- Tim Rea, CEO of Palringo at the time of our acquisition. Thank you for believing in us and validating what we had built.

Special Acknowledgements

- Melita Räsänen, our children's group nanny during their earliest years. Your dedication, knowledge, and care gave us peace of mind to focus on our work, knowing the home front was in excellent hands. Your advice made parenthood easier and more joyful.

A General Thank You

To the countless people who played a part in our journey - whether through advice, partnerships, or shared moments - you are remembered and deeply appreciated, even if not named individually here. Your contributions were invaluable.

Thank you all for being part of this adventure.

STARTUP TERMINOLOGY

- Angel investor: An individual or a small company that invests their own money into startups. Often, in addition to money, they give "sweat equity"—helping the startup move forward with their own network and expertise.
- Accelerator: A startup program that usually lasts from 3 weeks to 6 months and helps early-stage startups refine their ideas and get started. Often associated with a physical place where the startups work during the program.
- Burn rate: The speed at which you're burning cash. This is the most critical financial metric for a startup. If your burn rate is 10,000 EUR/month and you have 30,000 EUR in the bank, your runway is 3 months.
- MVP: Minimum Viable Product. The first version of the product that you launch and start to sell to customers. It's important to get the product to market as fast as you can—thus "Minimum"—but it also needs to be something that's already usable, hence "Viable."
- Pitch: The core idea of your startup presented clearly and concisely. A pitch is your first "sales line": what you do and why anyone should care. There are also official formats for pitches, ranging from 3 to 15 minutes. I like to think that everyone should know their own life's pitch: What makes you tick and why is that important to you?

- Pivot: A change in plans. This refers to any significant alteration in your product or business model. For example, you might develop for desktop instead of mobile, start selling to enterprises instead of consumers, or find a delivery channel that replaces your direct sales.
- PMF: Product-Market Fit. The point in time when your product fits a real market need and growth begins. Sales become easier, references increase, and customers start coming to you. It's time to start scaling.
- Runway: The amount of time a startup has left until the money runs out. A startup is like jumping off a cliff and assembling an airplane before hitting the ground. Runway is the time left for the airplane to be ready.
- Startup: A company that is still seeking a business model. A startup may have a product but is searching for a market that needs it, or it may understand a market need and is still building a product for that market.
- VC: Venture Capital fund. A fund that invests its money into startups. The sums invested by VCs are usually higher than those from angel investors. VCs get their money from Limited Partners (LPs).

ABOUT THE AUTHOR

Elina Arponen is a serial entrepreneur with over 20 years of experience in games and interactive media, and more than 15 years as a founder CEO. She has built, scaled, and exited. She is currently building Playables.ai, an AI-driven tool transforming how interactive ads and content are created. Elina brings a perspective that only comes from staying in the arena across multiple chapters of growth and reinvention.

In addition to her professional work, Elina enjoys spending time with her family, playing all kinds of games, reading, and travelling. These are all activities that take you on adventures.

TRIBE
STUDIOS

GARAGE
01/10/2016
PAY TO THE ORDER OF
StageCraft
5000
five thousand
Euros
Winner of Bootcamp
AVGarage

Thesaurus

VELVET
SUNDOWN
Stagecraftgames.com
Stories like you've never seen before, told by you.

VELVET SUNDOWN

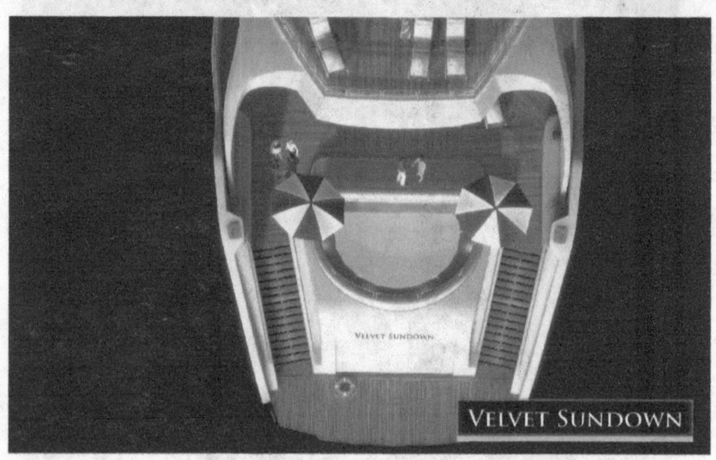
VELVET SUNDOWN
VELVET SUNDOWN

NASDAQ
JVC
SUPERMODELS
Panasonic

www.ingramcontent.com/pod-product-compliance
Lightning Source LLC
LaVergne TN
LVHW040221110826
845146LV00005B/1372

* 9 7 8 9 5 2 8 8 1 7 3 4 5 *